Disaster Proof
A Family Preparedness Guide

Shaun E. Allen

DEDICATION

To those that respond into danger and put their lives on the line for others, especially the personnel of Pasco County Fire Rescue….Thank you.

A special dedication to the United States Coast Guard crew of Station South Padre Island, 1998-2002. "Law and Order Along the Border" Hands down the best group of men and women I have ever had the pleasure of working with.

CONTENTS

ACKNOWLEDGMENTS

A special thanks is reserved for my wonderful wife Michelle. Without her example of hard work and dedication to higher learning I would not be in the position I am today that enabled me to write this book.

Knowledge is power. Information is liberating. Education is the premise of progress, in every society, in every family. –Kofi Annan (Ghanaian diplomat/2001 Nobel Peace Prize Winner)

1 INTRODUCTION: DISASTERS

What is a disaster? It can be a troublesome term to define. It is often defined in language too narrow or too broad, which can lead to disagreements on its actual meaning. What a disaster is to one person may not necessarily be the same to another due to different circumstances, such as socioeconomic situations. I feel that the easiest way to define it is: any event, natural or man-made, that causes damage and suffering, and requires some sort of outside assistance. This definition does have certain limitations as well; countries and regions can have different triggers for assistance and sometimes it can even be a political decision. For the purpose of this book, we will stick with a disaster being defined as any event that causes damage and suffering and requires outside assistance to the family unit.

A disaster can be caused by natural or man-made

events. Natural disasters can include weather events; such as hurricanes and floods, and geological events; such as earthquakes and volcanoes. Man-made disasters can include industrial, environmental, and transportation incidents, as well as terrorism. It is an ever-present reality that disasters, both natural and man-made, are on the rise globally. Natural disasters are striking with greater frequency and intensity. The pursuit of technology and new waves of terrorism is creating an atmosphere that increases the chance and scope of man-made disasters.

So why are disasters on the rise? It is inconsequential whether you believe the theory of man-made global warming or feel that climate change is a result of a cyclical global pattern; the truth of the matter is- climate change is real and it does have an effect on weather patterns. In addition, the never-ending pursuit of technological superiority often moves faster than safety standards can keep up with, which can increase the likelihood of an industrial type disaster, and terrorism is now breaking out of traditional geographical boundaries and is striking fear in many countries, including the United States. You must recognize that disasters can and do happen, regardless of the cause, and often affects individuals that think that such disasters could never reach them.

Many Americans live in an area where disasters,

specifically natural disasters, have the potential of causing great damage and loss. According to the Federal Emergency Management Agency (FEMA), flooding is the most prominent disaster in the United States. The statistics compiled by the National Flood Insurance Program (NFIP) show that there are a large number of people in the population that could be affected by flooding and that flood insurance claims between the years of 2002 and 2011 averaged over $2.9 billion per year. There are more and more people living in coastal regions and along many of the great rivers that are affected by hurricanes and other large rain events, which will increase the number of people involved in these flooding disasters. The United States is also unique with regard to tornados in that approximately 70% of all tornados that occur on earth rip right through the center of the country. These statistics are just a few of the reasons that highlight the importance for disaster preparedness. In your lifetime it is very possible that you and your family will be affected in some way by a disaster.

This book is designed to give guidance on basic emergency disaster preparedness to families in order to help them prepare for, and cope with disasters, and to increase their chances for survival when they do occur. This book is centered on an "all-hazards" approach and outlines specific preparedness activities that can be utilized in any disaster situation. The checklists presented can be adapted to fit any family unit and tailored for specific family needs. It is the goal of this book to give every family the knowledge and direction to better prepare for disasters and to help develop their own organized disaster plan with the specific goal of keeping the family unit safe and intact. This book is not a guide on specific disasters and emergencies and should not be treated as such, nor is it a "dooms day" preparation guide. It is strictly a guide to help families start the discussion of disaster preparedness and to give guidance to developing their own disaster action plan. There are many other "disaster guide" books out there that offer excellent information but can be quite overwhelming. They are designed as a reference book, but lets face it, I don't know of many individuals that will have these guide books in hand to reference during an actual disaster. Hopefully this book will give you information that is easy to remember and to apply so the need to have a "guide book" in hand is not necessary.

The last section of this book is dedicated to suggested activities that the family unit can do together to increase their knowledge and preparedness to make life a little easier when disasters do strike. Also, the Internet, the local emergency management office, and the local Red Cross organization are all great resources for information, so don't hesitate to utilize them to learn more about specific disasters that could affect your area.

A Note on Personal Responsibility

In the hours and days after a disaster strikes you and your family should be able to be self-sufficient without any outside help. Too many people in today's society hold the view that it is up to the government to provide preparedness and response to disasters when they happen. Families are often caught in the aftermath waiting sometimes up to a week or more for rescue and aid to reach them. This is especially true with very large disasters that involve many people and extreme weather conditions. You must understand that the first responders are going to be extremely overwhelmed in the immediate aftermath of a large disaster and despite their best efforts, may not be able to provide aid to your family for an extended period of time. The local, state and federal government all have important rolls in disaster preparedness and response but there still lies responsibility with that of the citizen to do everything that they can to prepare for and minimize the impact of a disaster on their household. An important aspect of this responsibility includes listening to local emergency managers and heeding their advice when it comes to actions that need to be taken prior to and during a disaster. This is especially important when mandatory evacuations are ordered. Remember, first responders will not respond during an active disaster if it is unsafe to do so. This is true of disasters that involve high winds and other hazardous conditions. The primary responsibility of first responders is scene safety and safety of their crew. They are no good to the response effort if they themselves become part of the disaster. First responders will remain in shelter until it is safe for them to start the post disaster response. This applies to any disaster whether it is manmade or a natural event.

Most large disasters are naturally occurring and many individuals that find themselves in need of rescuing during these disasters often have ample warning but fail to take the necessary precautions to get out of harms way. The best way to ensure that you and your family survive a disaster is to do everything you can to avoid being in one. There are, however, occasions when a disaster strikes with little or no warning and the importance of a disaster action plan for your family becomes extremely clear. Throughout the rest of this book you will find helpful information and guidance to prepare you and your family for any disaster event-- so get comfortable, grab a pen (pages for note taking in the back) and start taking the steps to become

DISASTER PROOF.

2 THE ACTION OF INACTION

What causes inaction during disasters and emergencies? There are many reasons that individuals choose not to take action in these situations. Some individuals do not act because of fear or lack of knowledge and are scared that the result of their action will be unsuccessful. This is often seen in emergency situations where bystanders do not act because they don't know what to do and are afraid that if they do get involved, their actions could add to the problem. While working as a firefighter/paramedic, I often responded to scenes where it was reported that an individual was unconscious or not breathing only to find several bystanders at the patient's side with the desire to do something but lacked the knowledge of what to do- and therefore, were paralyzed by fear. The more knowledge that an individual has about a disaster or emergency, the more likely they are to take action when the disaster or emergency presents itself. There are other individuals that do not take action because they fail recognize the danger or potential for danger and by the time an action is needed, it is often to late. This latter group of individuals is who this section is focused on. The statement *"it will never happen to me"* is a dangerous one to make. I'm sure the countless car crashes and house fires that I responded to involved several individuals that woke up that day not thinking anything traumatic was going to happen to them. I am not saying that you should live in fear and "expect" something terrible to happen. That being said, you must also be cognizant of the fact that you are not immune from a disaster no matter how big or small. There are those that have the attitudes that a certain disaster will not happen just because it has never happened before, or has been so long since the last occurrence. They have a false sense of security that the trend will continue. This can be dangerous, not only for preparation purposes, but also when it comes time to heed warnings.

Many individuals that live along the East coast of Florida remember the devastation that Hurricane Andrew unleashed in 1992. When there are hurricane advisories and warnings in this area, many individuals do take notice and will evacuate. Compare that to areas like the Northeast along the Jersey Shore and New York. There have been very few strong storms to reach this area. Hurricane Irene skirted up the east coast in 2011 causing local emergency managers to issue evacuation orders. The storm fortunately did not live up to the expected hype but set the stage for something more dangerous. A year later when "Superstorm Sandy" approached the same area, many did not evacuate because they expected the same result. There are mixed theories of why people in different geographical regions treat evacuations differently. Some say it is the "crying wolf" syndrome; where many false alarms can result in disregarding such warnings. The Sandy incident is a tough one to fit into this mold. Irene was the only recent storm that caused an evacuation order to be issued and despite the overhype, was not necessarily a complete dud. Flooding still occurred and there was damage to several homes and businesses. There were not multiple "false alarms" that would constitute the "crying wolf" syndrome as a reason for the lack of evacuations in the Sandy case. In addition, having multiple false alarms does not necessarily mean a change in the percentages of people that do evacuate. There have been many false alarms in Florida communities due to the ever-changing hurricane spaghetti models that forecast the expected landfall of such storms. These can change sometimes by the hour and cause several different communities to start evacuating only to have the major effects of the storm to miss them completely. This was seen during several Florida storms in the 1980's that affected Panama City Beach. There was a series of storms that caused evacuation of the city multiple times and yet the number of people that evacuated remained almost the same each time. I feel that the number of people that evacuate can be related to how many of them have actually seen the devastation caused by these large disaster events. Florida has seen it's share of hurricane destruction and more people tend to heed evacuation orders as opposed to many individuals that live along the coast of the northeast. I understand that there are many other factors involved, like socioeconomic factors, but the fact remains that frequent disasters can often result in a more "willingness to cooperate" attitude. It is troublesome that society only learns lessons after something devastating happens.

Whether you live in an area where disasters can occur frequently or in an area where there has not been a large disaster for decades, you must still take *action* by preparing and heeding the warnings issued by your local emergency management office.

A Word on Mitigation and Preparedness

The need to recognize the potential for a disaster and to take steps to minimize the effects of the disaster if it does occur is the basic principle in disaster mitigation and preparedness. Every level of government, from the local to the federal level, engages in these mitigation and preparedness activities. For example, your family may live in an area that is prone to flooding. It is likely that the local government has developed some type of mitigation and preparedness program to minimize the potential for flooding and to also minimize the damage if flooding does occur. The local government had to first understand that there was a potential for flooding and then had to develop plans and programs to help minimize the risk. We are going to take these same principles and apply them in the family unit in order to prepare your family in the event of a disaster.

As a family unit, you must indentify the most common disasters that have, or may occur in your area. This is a great activity to do as a family to get the discussion started about disasters and disaster preparedness. These disasters might include: flooding, tornados, earthquakes, tsunami, fires, snowstorms, severe droughts, volcanic eruptions, industrial incidents, terrorism or a combination of several of these disasters. Various disasters can strike at any given time but it is a reality that some areas of the earth are more prone to certain disasters than others. The goal of the activity is--as a family unit, you identify the potential for a disaster. This is the most important step in going from inaction to action. Once your family identifies and discusses different disasters that might be encountered, it is time to start laying down the framework for preparedness. This starts with developing a general disaster action plan. The great thing about developing a disaster plan is that the basic plan will cover most disaster situations, both expected and unexpected. This is not to say that you shouldn't tailor certain aspects of your disaster plan to meet specific issues of specific disasters, but many components of a disaster plan overlap to encompass any situation. The steps of how to develop the plan will be covered in chapter seven.

It is a good practice to gather information from your local emergency management or Red Cross office on the specific disasters that are common in your area and incorporate the suggested actions into your own disaster action plan. Once you have a plan established, the next step is to practice. The saying "practice makes perfect" definitely applies here. You can parallel this with a sports team. A team can sit down and talk about how they are going to play the game but unless they actually practice, chances are that their actual playing ability will not meet up to what they discussed. As a family, a couple of times a year, you should review you disaster action plan and actually "go through the motions" of running through your plan. This is very important with families that have small children. The more practice that these small children have, the more likely it is that they will perform well when there is an actual emergency. Remember all of the fire drills that you went through when you were in elementary school? I know this may seem silly and over the top but TRUST me…you do not want to rely on your written plan to be followed in an actual emergency if it has never been practiced or walked through. Walking through the motions of the disaster plan is also important in that it allows you as a family to identify any shortfalls in the plan and to adjust accordingly. Something may have not gone as well as you had planned and it is much better to identify and fix the problem during the practice than to wait until an actual emergency.

3 SPECIAL NEEDS

Special needs in context of this book will deal with any out of the ordinary situations that could potentially add to the difficulty of disaster preparedness. This can include, but not limited to, lack of mobility, income level, lack of access to resources, medical conditions requiring specialized medicine, pets, and age of persons involved. Many disasters have shown how the lack of planning for groups with special needs can have devastating consequences. Hurricane Katrina proved to be especially devastating on these individuals because many were left at the mercy of the storm. The elderly, people living in poverty, and many pet owners were not considered in the coordination of the mass evacuations taking place all through New Orleans and surrounding areas, and consequently were left behind;

many of these individuals died as a result of this oversight and poor planning.

Lack of Mobility

There are various reasons why someone might be lacking in mobility and can include injury, disability, and age issues. This type of special need should be identified from the onset and addressed during planning. This might require someone from your family being assigned to assist getting the person with limited mobility to safety when the need arises. This might also only be a temporary situation as in the case of someone on crutches due to a broken leg. When these situations arise, it is important that you amend the disaster action plan accordingly. Exits might need to be modified to allow for easy egress from the structure during an emergency situation. Planning for sheltering in place might need to be adjusted to allow for easy access to safe areas within the home itself. Whatever the reason for the mobility issue, steps must be taken in advance to make it as easy and as efficient as possible for these individuals when the need arises that they must change locations or seek shelter.

Income Level and Lack of Access to Resources

Unfortunately, many of the individuals that are most affected by disasters are the ones that struggle on a day-to-day basis already. They often do not have the means to spend extra money on preparation and many do not have transportation to get out harms way. Many have no insurance and lack any significant financial security. There are different levels of economical struggles and if you find that you can not afford many of the basic preparation resources, don't give up. Contact your local emergency management or Red Cross office. They may have area or regional programs that can assist you in preparedness. It might even bring awareness to an issue on community preparedness that these decision and policy makers might be able to effect a positive change in order to better prepare the community.

Medical Conditions

Many of us have family members that have certain medical conditions that are easily handled on a day-to-day basis. We are able to control these conditions with a variety of medications and expert consultations. Some of us even fulfill the role of primary care giver. Disasters can make these medical conditions an almost insurmountable challenge due to the nature of disasters and how they disrupt even the simplest task of daily life. Several considerations must be made with regard to individuals with medical conditions. Questions to ask:

Does the medical condition require specialized medication?

Does the medication require special handling? (i.e. refrigeration)

Could the medical condition be exacerbated due to the nature of the disaster?

Does the individual require frequent doctor visits? (i.e. dialysis)

Question as many things as possible and "what if" everything. Try to think of as many issues that could arise due to a disaster scenario and have contingencies in place.

During disasters electrical power is often taken out, roads can be impassable for days at a time, and the stress of a disaster can have negative impacts on many diseases and illnesses that are present in humans. Family members with medical conditions need careful consideration in your disaster action plan. Arrangements should be made to have enough medications to carry them through until help can arrive. There should be plans to keep medications cool if they are required to be refrigerated. Notice should also be given to local emergency managers or first responders of the need for a family member requiring frequent doctor visits or special medical assistance as seen in patients requiring dialysis, special respiratory care, or any other unique medical need. Having this knowledge ahead of time can help focus their efforts to ensure that this need is met as fast as reasonably possible when a disaster occurs. I speak from experience during my emergency services career when I say that having information about special medical needs of individuals in our first due response area helped us better prepare to meet those needs whatever the emergency. This information often came in the form of a nicely written letter by a family member explaining the particular medical situation and also included the address, contact information, and sometimes a picture of the individual needing special attention. We also enjoyed when these individuals would visit the fire house so we could get to know them personally and to address any questions or concerns that they had. Families with special medical needs issues, no matter how big or small, must be proactive to ensure that these needs are met during a disaster situation.

Pets and Animals

One of the most frustrating things that I encountered while working both in the United States Coast Guard and as a firefighter paramedic was interacting with individuals with pets that refused to evacuate to a shelter because the shelter did not accept pets. If your family owns a pet you can probably relate to this mentality because it is like leaving behind a family member. Many would rather stay in a dangerous situation rather than leave a loved one behind. It is imperative that you make arrangements prior to a disaster for your pets. You may have to do a little research to find out which shelters or locations are pet friendly. Many require that you have crates for your pets as well as other safety items like muzzles. Pets can pose a safety risk to others because they will often act very defensive due to their protective nature as well as being scared and confused. The good news is that more and more emergency planners are taking pets into consideration and shelters are starting to make accommodations for pets. In addition, don't discount the willingness of family members that live outside of the disaster area to take in your pet or pets. Again, this should be discussed and pre-arranged prior to a disaster. Considerations for your pet should be made the same as you would for a person in your house hold. You want to ensure that you have enough food and water for the animal as well as any medications that they might require. (You do not want your pet to be taking away from your daily food and water intake) You also want to ensure that you have a body harness for dogs and cats along with a muzzle and strong leash. If the predetermined shelter does not provide crating, you will have to procure a crate suitable for your pet. It is also a good idea to have the contact information for your vet incase of an injury or illness that might occur as a result of the disaster.

Farms or properties that house a large number of animals must also make prior arrangements for the possible evacuation or sheltering in place of their animals. This can be quite the challenge especially with properties that house large animals or very large numbers of animals. Horse farms, cattle farms, goat farms, and properties with exotic species of animals all fall into this category. For example, there is a property in close proximity of a firehouse that I worked out of that is a family owned "zoo" that specializes in "exotic animal" rescue-- specifically large CATS. This place houses a black leopard, African lions, jaguars, Bengal tigers, bears, and various monkeys. Many of the cats are housed in natural areas that are surrounded by fence. This particular geographical region is prone to wildfires, severe thunderstorms, and during the hurricane season, can be affected by high winds and torrential rains. This type of facility would definitely want to have a back up plan if they needed to move these animals as a result of an impending or occurring disaster. Could you imagine if these animals were accidently released into the surrounding areas during or after a disaster? What kind of fear would this place on the population especially with the inevitable overwhelming media coverage? Visions of the 1996 movie *The Ghost and the Darkness,* which was a fictionalized account of two lions that attacked and killed workers during the building of the 1989 African Uganda-Mombasa Railway, would be replaying in the minds eye…well, at least for those that have seen the movie. You do not have to own a "zoo" to have exotic animals that would require specialized housing. Many individuals own birds, snakes, and other reptiles that may require special handling and attention during a disaster. I will never forget the house fire I responded to that had a large fish tank in the living room. After putting the fire out we were engaged in salvage operations when I decided to check and see if any of the "fish" had made it. The tank was black with soot and was overflowing with heated water as a result of the firefighting activities. I nonchalantly lifted the cover only to be greeted by an extremely irritated, extremely large, Nile monitor! If you don't know what that is--do an Internet search. You will see why I was always very cautious after that incident when checking on the family's "fish" after a fire.

All animals, pets or otherwise, rely on their owners for food, water, and their safety and well-being. It is not fair to these animals that they are left at the mercy of a disaster because their owner was not responsible and failed to take the proper precautions to make arrangements to ensure their safety. It is also not fair to your family and loved ones by putting yourself in danger because you choose not to evacuate due to poor planning and not making prior arrangements to be able to take your pet with you.

Age of Persons Involved

Many families have individuals that are both young and elderly living under one roof. Many of these individuals may encounter other special needs seen in the afore mentioned issues, such as mobility and medical concerns. Many of these individuals rely on others for their well-being. The stress of the disaster is often amplified in this population and their coping mechanisms may not handle the effects of disasters as well as middle-aged individuals. Discussing disasters and having an easy to follow action plan established could help minimize the fear and anxiety that this population often feels. Being mindful of their needs during the planning process will help ensure their safety.

Somewhat related to mobility, but is included in this section, is the ability of this population to get out of the house if a situation arises where it is warranted. Many two story family homes have the children's bedrooms on the top floor. In the event of a fire or first floor flooding, the normal means of egress (front door) may not be an option. There are several commercial devices that can be purchased to enable escape from a second level window but must be age appropriate and training on how to use the devices must be completed. Implementing one of these devices will be something that you and your family will have to discuss. Remember, the nearest exit may not be the front door. A good fire safety class is recommended for the entire family to attend. Escaping the home in times of an emergency is just one of many topics that are usually covered in these types of classes.

The elderly in the home often have their own little section of the house. Many families build additions in order to accommodate these family members. It is a good idea to include a means of egress to the outside directly from these additions. Even modifying an existing room with an exit may be warranted. It is much easier for elderly individuals to get out of structures if they have direct access to the outside. It can be difficult for some of them if they have to ambulate any distance to reach an exit, especially those routes that include going up or down stairs.

Including both of these age groups in the planning process will give them a sense of control and importance and will make it more likely that they will follow the plan when a disaster does strike. There are many individuals, both young and old alike, that seem to have a more grounded sense of reality and a better head on their shoulders than many middle aged adults so don't discount their input, it could be the difference between life and death!

4 THE PLAN AND THE COMMUNITY

Talking about formulating a disaster action plan is not enough…you must put it down in writing and practice. Organization in every day life enables one to be efficient, minimize confusion, and allow for easy adaptation when problems are encountered. Having an organized plan for a disaster is no different. Some may call your initiative in planning overkill or just being paranoid… let them; when a disaster strikes, you do not want the opinions of these people to be the reason that you were not prepared. It has been my experience that disaster planning is often on the minds of many friends and neighbors but they may not know where to begin. Including your neighbors and friends can be a great way to open up other resources that you might have not otherwise had access to. By you formulating a plan and sharing your plan with others can get the preverbal ball rolling and can lead to a whole block or community being better prepared to face a disaster. Get out and meet your neighbors! Suburbia has turned into a 9 to 5 job force that seems to enter and exit the world through a magical portal called a garage door. Many individuals do not know much about their neighbors other than what time they leave and get home from work. Do you know if you could rely on your neighbor during a disaster? Or, do you know if your neighbor would need assistance if a disaster were to strike? This age of closed doors and "go it alone" attitudes is very dangerous in the face of these increasing disasters. Communities are built of different families and we should not wait until a disaster strikes before "we come together" as a community. We should know our neighbors and what makes our communities tick, and as a community, work on family disaster preparedness. Local community centers are a great place to hold gatherings a couple times a year to discuss disaster preparedness to ensure that not only your family is prepared, but also the families of your neighbors. It may take a little initiative on your part to help get your community better prepared, but you have already shown more initiative than the average person by taking an interest and reading this book. The good news is that you can usually find one or two other families in a community that are just as interested in disaster preparedness and can help with these types of community events. It is a great way to organize the community and pull resources together with disaster preparedness in mind. Many communities have volunteer groups that will assist the citizens in times of a disaster and can encompass anything from communications to first aid. The point is, you must first understand your community and get to know your neighbors before you can lead a successful campaign of disaster preparedness. You can also reach out to you local emergency manager. The local office of emergency management is more than willing to provide information that can help your community better prepare for disasters. They will often give free classes and training to interested parties. They are also able to get volunteer groups involved, like the Red Cross, to not only recruit new volunteers, but also offer training on how to better prepare for specific disasters. The better prepared your community is, the more resilient it will be when there is a disaster.

5 THE DOME EFFECT

Imagine your property in a futuristic time period in which there is a large dome type shield that extends over your house from property line to property line. This dome is responsible for the protection of your property and home from all dangers. Nothing can get through it…water, fire, and wind have no effect. Not a plausible scenario? It may not be feasible to construct such a structure but I offer the idea that you can establish a virtual type of dome that will help protect your home, both inside and out, from the afore mentioned elements. It starts with doing a risk assessment of your property. You do not need to have 100 acres in order to utilize these principles. It can be a very small piece of property or even an apartment in an apartment building-- the principles remain the same. You must first identify specific hazards on your property.

Obvious ones are trees overhanging the house, dead trees on the property, poor water drainage, and thick underbrush and vegetation that extends close to the house. Many of these problems you could address yourself but it is always a good idea to hire professionals to assist especially when it comes to clearing trees that are near to your house. It would be a pretty awful scenario if you wanted to clear the large tree that extended over your roof in fear that a storm could cause it to fall and damage your home only for you yourself to make a wrong cut and help that nightmare come true without the storm. Falling trees in high wind or heavy snow conditions can cause much of the damage to homes during natural disasters so it is important to take care of these issues before hand. There are also many homes lost to wildfires where the wildland/urban interface occurs. This is the area right at the edge of communities where the land turns back into its natural state. During a wildfire, fire can spread very quickly through this natural vegetation and can extend into communities in the form of house fires if there is not a buffer zone. In wildland firefighting this buffer zone is often referred to as a defensible space. It is an area around your home that is free of fuel, like brush and high grass, which a quickly spreading wildfire will consume. Remember, a fire is always looking for fuel to continue burning. You take away the fuel...you stop the fire.

This maintaining of the property around your home can extend to the actual structure of the home itself. You need to ensure that the gutter systems are free of leaves and dirt, not only for fire combustion issues, but also to alleviate problems with drainage and water damage. Inspect the roof to ensure that there is no damage to the shingles or other roof coverings. Many of these issues go unnoticed until a heavy rain and wind event when water starts pouring into the home. It is a good practice to inspect your property and home at least once a year to help identify and correct issues.

Having all of your important homeowner's insurance documents in order is just as important as physically taking steps to protect your property. Many people often overlook this important aspect and are quit surprised to learn what their homeowner's insurance does or does not cover. It is very important that you go over your policy with your insurance company to ensure that you know exactly what the terms of the policy are. For example, water damage coverage may or may not cover run off or surface water that enters your home due to heavy rain. If the water entered through a damaged portion of the roof, you would be covered, but since it hit the ground it is now considered surface water...you may not be covered, especially if you do not have flood protection in your policy. Individuals that I know that are in the insurance business tell me that it is amazing how many people do not know what is in their policy and that it is a terrible situation to have to explain to them that their insurance did not cover the damaged caused by a disaster due to a lack of coverage. It is also a good idea to inventory everything in your house to assist insurance adjusters in the event that your home is completely destroyed due to a disaster. According to my friend Charlie, an experienced insurance claims adjuster, at a minimum you should take photos of every room and its contents. An accompanying written log of the items and their value is also a good idea. The best practice is to video record every room while talking about the items and their values. This information should be secured in an off-site location that is easily accessible after a disaster. Insurance adjusters cannot make items up, they can only reimburse you for what items that you can remember were present in your home. Having this cataloged inventory of your possessions will help ensure that you are compensated by the insurance companies when a disaster strikes and destroys your possessions. Trust me…it can save you days or weeks worth of headaches. Whether you like insurance companies or despise them--insurance is a must have and the better you understand your policy, the better you will be able to make informed changes to it to help insure that you have the most appropriate coverage.

Protecting these insurance documents is also very important. You should invest in a fire and waterproof lock box to secure them in. All important documents should be kept in this fashion. This can include social security cards, banking information, birth certificates, travelers checks/emergency cash, and any other similar important documents. It is also a good practice to make several copies of these documents (EXCLUDING THE MONEY!) and securing them in other places, especially the photos or video cataloged inventory of your possessions. A safety deposit box at a bank can be obtained annually for a nominal fee and is a great place to secure copies of these important items. However, banks will often be inaccessible during and after a large disaster so make sure you are securing documents that you won't necessarily need in the few days following a disaster. Some individuals have a personal safe at their place of work and is also an excellent location to secure important documents. Today's technology can also allow you to store encrypted digital files that can be accessed anywhere from a computer. This can prove to be very useful in large disasters when access to physical storage locations might be an issue.

There are other universal safety and preparedness items that every home needs that will add to the overall safety of the family. Coming from a firefighting background, the obvious for me are smoke detectors and fire extinguishers. These items can be life saving in various different disaster scenarios. Fires can start due to many different reasons, especially during disasters involving structural damage and downed power lines. Smoke detectors can alert you of a life-threatening situation involving a fire that is developing in another part of the house. This audible warning can give you enough advance notice that allows you to make it out of the structure safely. There should be a detector placed in all rooms and common areas. Fire extinguishers should be placed in easy accessible areas and are most commonly kept in the kitchen, garage, or utility closet. The extinguishers should be type ABC, which refers to the type of fire they are suitable for- A=(trash, paper, wood) B=(flammable liquid) and C=(electrical). If your home has multiple floors, insure that there are extinguishers on each level.

A back-up power supply or generator should be considered, especially in those areas that are prone to severe storms that can cause frequent power outages. These items can be expensive but are a wise investment when it comes to heating/cooling your home or keeping power to your refrigerator in order to keep your food from spoiling. Remember to follow all of the safety precautions that come with these generators. There are several people killed each year because they disregard safety instructions and operated these generators inside of their homes or garages. This is a very dangerous practice due to the carbon monoxide exposure and the potential for death that can result from this action. There are also fire safety issues encountered when the generators need to be refueled. It is important to turn the motor off and let it cool down. A hot engine can cause the fuel and fumes to ignite and make a bad situation a lot worse. Make sure you check the level of engine oil every time you refuel. Taking time to ensure that the proper level of fluids are present will minimize the chance for an engine failure and can add many years to the life of your investment.

6 THE DISASTER KIT

Having all of your disaster preparedness items organized and in one or two locations can be extremely helpful when chaos ensues during or after a disaster. Ideally this supply cache should be stored in an easy to access location and should be contained in a carry friendly container. Many people designate a closet or other small room to store these items and will usually put them in bags/backpacks or plastic containers that can be easily removed if the need arises and it becomes necessary to leave the house. The goal is to have these items easily accessible, in quantities that will let you be self sufficient for several days or more, and to have some way of taking items with you if you need to flee your residents. There are many commercial disaster kits available but they can be quite expensive. I find that it is much easier to put these kits together yourself so you will have control of what is in them and minimize the often useless items that come in many commercial packages. The following sections will highlight items that you should consider having but is by no means an all-inclusive list. The following will include three sections comprising of food/water, first aid, and general disaster supplies. Feel free to add or take away from the suggested inclusions to meet your individual needs. The following suggestions are a great start if you are unsure where to begin or what to include. Having these basic items will make your situation much better in the event of a disaster. Your family will thank you!

Food and Water

The most important aspect of disaster survival is your ability to prepare for an extended period of time without being able to replenish your food and water supply. FEMA suggests that you have at least 1 gallon of water per person per day in order to sustain them for three days. This is a minimum that you should have stored at any given time. It is a good idea to prepare for a longer period of time especially if a known disaster is looming as in the case of a hurricane, winter storm, or period of forecasted extreme weather. I suggest that when you are aware of a potential disaster that you have enough water for each individual of your household to last at least seven days. This means 7 gallons of water per person. This may seem like a lot but if you are isolated from rescue or aid because of a large disaster you will be glad that you took the steps to ensure that you had the extra water. It may not be feasible to carry all of this water with you if the need arises that you must leave your home. I suggest that you purchase backpack's that have built in water bladders or places to attach or carry water bottles. I am an advocate for Kelty bags due to their large carrying capacities and weight distribution abilities. It is up to you to determine what is best for your family, but remember…water is the most important item post disaster. Humans can only survive a few days without it so don't cut corners here. You should NEVER drink storm or flood water due to the contaminants that could be present.

Food can either make a bad situation bearable or make it seem even worse. In the Coast Guard, especially while underway at sea, food was seen as a morale booster. Individuals that were at sea for extended patrols often ate very well. I was attached to a small boat station and it was hit or miss with the food, but I can remember meeting up with a 270-foot patrol boat for a 3-day drug patrol out in the middle of the Gulf of Mexico and being amazed at the food they had. The first dinner I ate on that patrol was a filet mignon cooked just the way I like it, rare! Everyone on that patrol with me thoroughly enjoyed the meals, except for the one individual that was seasick the entire time due to the heavy seas that we were in. A diet of saltine crackers and water was in order for him. The point of this story is to highlight how food can be a source of comfort and morale when in difficult situations. Being at sea, away from family, in rough conditions, can sometimes make one feel like they are stranded on a floating island. Having unique and good food gives you something to look forward to and can help suppress some of the anxiety and depression that can often creep in during difficult situations. Keep that principle in mind when choosing food for your disaster kit. Obviously you will want to look for foods that do not spoil and have a good shelf life. They should be calorie heavy without being overly high in fat and sugar. Most nutrition stores and grocery stores carry products that can be used as meal replacements that many heath conscious individuals utilize on a daily basis. These are usually packed with vitamins and sustained energy. You can try a variety of different ones to figure out which are the best for you. Many of these come in bar form and take up very little space, which can be useful when you have to pack up and leave your home. Canned foods are also a good option because of their extended shelf life. Make sure you have a manual can opener and keep it with the kit. You do not want to have a shelf full of can goods with the only opener being an electric one. This can make for a frustrating situation when you are hungry and can't open any of your food when there is no power. If you have food in your refrigerator and freezer, make sure you utilize these items first as they will spoil very quickly if the power goes out. Cooking my be an issue but can be accomplished with a simple gas or charcoal grill. Some individuals purchase small camping grills for their kits and can be carried in a bag if you have to evacuate your house. I would suggest limiting the weight that you will have to carry and only take the food items that do not require cooking. Water at that point will be more important than the ability to cook food and the extra weight of a portable grill.

First Aid

The ability to manage injuries during a disaster can literally be the difference between life and death. This section is not a first aid course but I will cover some basic information that you should know in order to deal with one of the more common injuries seen in disaster situations (lacerations and bleeding) and basic first aid equipment that you should include in your disaster kit. You and your family should seriously consider taking a basic first aid and cardio pulmonary resuscitation (CPR) course. This course can give the proper training and information to handle a variety of emergency problems. The skills and knowledge gained in these classes are great to have not only for disaster situations, but you may never know when these skills will be called upon to help save someone's life during day-to-day activities. While working on the rescue, there are several individuals that we transported to the emergency room that are walking around today as a result of the actions taken by bystanders prior to our arrival; they had taken a basic first aid and CPR course.

The great thing about the human body is that it is very resilient. It can take quite a beating and still function relatively well. During my time working in emergency services I have seen horrific injuries and was amazed how well the human body was able to cope. The God given defensive mechanisms that are present in every human enables the body to compensate for a period of time after major traumatic events. This is commonly seen in traumatic injuries involving lacerations and bleeding. The body will automatically constrict blood vessels to minimize the blood loss and to divert more blood to the central core where the vital organs are located. The body also releases different factors that start the clotting process, further reducing the amount of bleeding. This buys the individual some time until medical attention can be sought out. Many of the injuries that are seen in large disaster situations involve lacerations. It is important that you know how to assist the body in slowing down the bleeding. The average adult contains around 5-6 liters of blood and in the presence of heavy bleeding, it does not take long to deplete that volume. The most basic treatment for heavy bleeding is direct pressure. This can be accomplished by physically holding a towel or thick trauma gauze pad directly over the wound. Once a towel or gauze pad is in place, you never want to remove it since in can disrupt any clotting process that has started. If the blood is continuing to bleed through the covering, you just keep adding more towels or gauze and increase the pressure. A constricting bandage (ACE bandage) can assist in creating adequate pressure to slow bleeding. Elevation can also be used in conjunction with direct pressure to help slow or stop bleeding. This is useful in large lacerations to the extremities (arms and legs). The goal is to get the injured extremity above the level of the heart. If the laceration is on your arm, you can hold it above your head to help control the bleeding. If the laceration is on your leg, you may have to lay on the floor and hold your leg up or place it on an elevated surface to achieve the desired result. In very rare occasions, bleeding from an extremity may not be able to be controlled by direct pressure and elevation alone. A more aggressive procedure may be required in the form of a tourniquet. A tourniquet should be made of a one to two inch wide piece of material that can be tied a few inches above the uncontrolled bleeding site. This cuts the blood flow off to the injured area completely and should only be used as a LAST RESORT. Although it will slow or stop the bleeding, the result is often the loss of the affected extremity.

I cannot stress enough the importance of taking a first aid and CPR course. It is not my intent to give a first aid lesson in this book but I wanted to give a quick overview of lacerations because they are very common in disasters. However, in reality, these types of soft tissue injuries are often accompanied with other injuries like fractures and burns. By taking a first aid and CPR course you will gain the confidence to be able to take care of yourself and family when a disaster strikes.

Part of treating injuries during a disaster is having the equipment to do so. There are many commercial first aid kits available but they can be very expensive. Like disaster kits, they often contain items that are not necessarily very useful. I feel that it is better to build your own first aid kit so you can customize it and get the type and quantity of materials that you want. You may have to shop around to find deals on supplies and the Internet can be a great resource. Keep in mind that many medical first aid supplies can have expiration dates. You want to inspect your first aid kit annually to insure that you have no items that have expired.

The following checklist is made of items that I suggest you obtain for your kit. This is not an all-inclusive list but it will insure that you have the basics. It is the minimum that I feel comfortable with having in my first aid kit. As you gain training and knowledge, you can add to this list. You can just check off the items in the book itself or utilize the list as a guide as you make your own list for your kit. It is important that you place these items in an easy to access container and keep it organized. There are several medical bags that you can purchase but a medium sized plastic container with a lid will work well also. Some individuals often utilize a tackle box for this purpose. These can be found at most stores that carry fishing equipment. Many tackle boxes have separate plastic containers that people use to fashion their own easy to carry and accessible first aid kit. You just need to experiment to find what works best for you.

Suggested Checklist for a First Aid Kit

☐ *Various sizes of gauze pads and trauma dressings*. These can be used to assist in bleeding control from lacerations and to help cover wounds such as burns.

☐ *1 and 2 inch rolls of cloth tape*. These can be useful in helping secure bandages over wounds and securing splits for fractures.

☐ *1 and 2 inch rolls of plastic tape*. Same uses as above but seem to work better in climates containing a lot of moisture.

☐ *Various sizes of band-aids and steri-strips*. These are useful to cover small wounds and cuts or to help close larger wounds to aid in bleeding control.

☐ *Roller bandages Kling/Kerlix*. These can be used to hold dressings in place. They also allow you the ability to apply more pressure to bleeding sites by tightly wrapping the bandage over the dressing and wound.

☐ *Triangle (cravat) slings*. These are triangle shaped bandage that can have multiple uses. They are primarily used to fashion a sling to support shoulder or clavicle (collarbone) injuries.

☐ *Ace-Bandage.* This can help you fashion a pressure bandage due to its constrictive nature. It can also aid in giving support to weakened joints as a result of injury.

☐ *Mild soap.* This can be used to clean minor wounds and help prevent infections. **NOTE-** What about hydrogen peroxide you ask? Using peroxide to clean wounds can actually destroy healthy tissue making the healing process more difficult. It is better to use cool water and the mild soap.

☐ *Sterile water or Normal Saline.* This can be used to flush and clean wounds and can be especially useful to help get foreign particles out of the eyes.

☐ *Antibiotic ointment.* This will help keep minor wounds moist to promote healing. It can also reduce the likelihood that dressings will stick to the wound. Also, being an antibiotic, it can reduce the chance of infection.

☐ *Blunt ended scissors.* They can be utilized to cut bandages and dressings to size or to expose injury sites by cutting clothing.

Other items that should be considered are dependent on the families that are going to be utilizing it. Any medications that are specific for certain family members should be labeled and included in the kit. It is important to try to have at least a weeks worth of these medications in reserve. Other medication, such as Tylenol or Advil is also a good idea to include in these kits. They can aid in pain relief of minor aches and pains, which can be intensified during a disaster. Make sure you place a "medical chart" in the first aid kit that list all allergies, prescribed medications, and known medical problems of family members. First responders will need this information if they are called upon to assist you during a disaster.

Miscellaneous Gear

The amount of gear that you want to store for your disaster needs is ultimately up to you and your family. I feel that there is definitely a limit on the amount of gear that you can reasonably store in preparation for a disaster…too much gear can sometimes be a hindrance, especially if you are trying to take it with you if you have to evacuate. I suggest that if you want to secure a large amount of gear that you separate it into two different sections. One for sheltering in place and the other to quickly grab and carry out if you must evacuate. This alleviates the need to decide what to bring and what to leave behind when conditions during a disaster are rapidly deteriorating.

Miscellaneous gear that I strongly suggest you place in your disaster kits includes tarps, whistles, flashlights, batteries, sanitation and hygiene supplies, extra clothing for inclement weather, and several changes of socks.

Tarps are very useful in many different situations. They can be utilized to cover holes in walls or roofs during or post disaster that will help keep the elements out. They are also great for making a make shift shelter if you ever have to leave your home and are caught outside in the elements. You can search the Internet and find a thousand different uses for a tarp…it is quite impressive.

Whistles are often overlooked but they can be a lifesaving piece of equipment. If you are stranded or trapped, the whistle can be utilized to project an audible sound that can be heard great distances. This is especially true if you are ever trapped under rubble or other debris. There should be a whistle for everyone in the family and should be on some type of lanyard that can be kept on their person at all times for the duration of the disaster event. Make sure the whistle is marine grade and is able to get wet. Some whistles utilize a cork type substance as the whistle ball and can swell when wet, rendering the whistle useless. Waterproof whistles can be found online and in most water sports stores.

Flashlights and batteries can be very valuable when you are stumbling around the house when the power is out. These are items that you want to check a couple of times a year because batteries and bulbs can go bad. I have one flashlight that self-charges when you shake it. It utilizes a magnetic field to charge an internal rechargeable battery pack. It can be a pain to use for a long period of time but it is great in a pinch when all else fails. I also suggest that you place flashlights in various places throughout your house because you can never know where you will be when you suddenly need one. Also, ensure that you have water proof matches and a lighter for lighting candles and starting fires in order to cook with or to keep warm.

Sanitation and hygiene supplies are essential not only for comfort, but for health and safety as well. All of your preparation could be for not if you become ill because you failed to prepare for the necessary sanitation and hygiene issues. These supplies should include household chlorine bleach, soap, and hand sanitizer. Sanitation is an issue during disasters especially when there is flooding. You want to ensure that the area that you are sheltering in remains clean. Any eating utensils and drinking containers should be as clean and as sanitized as possible. You should clean your hands often and refrain from putting them near your mouth and eyes. Hygiene supplies can include plastic garbage bags, toilet paper, baby wipes, toothpaste, toothbrush, floss, deodorant, etc. You must be especially careful when disposing of human waste. Toilets may not be operating if water pumps lack power or if there is significant damage to plumbing or sewage systems. Primitive camping techniques require you to dig a hole (catholes) at least 6-8 inches deep in the ground so that you can completely cover the human waste with dirt when you are done. There are times when you might not be able go outside and an alternative option will be required. The most common way to alleviate this problem is via a bucket with a tight fitting lid or some of the more expensive portable disaster toilets. Granted, either option is not a fun one but they will make life much better if you are confined to a small shelter for an extended period of time.

Clothing for inclement weather is dependent on where you live. If you are expecting a winter storm, cold weather gear and clothes that you can easily layer will be more important than sun hats and SPF rated lightweight clothing. Make sure you store the extra clothing in a water tight container to help protect them. I find that the vacuum sealable plastic storage bags are useful for this purpose not only because it helps save space, but it also helps in keeping moisture out. I also have a variety of "dry bags" that I use when kayaking. These too can serve the purpose of storing extra clothing in due to their waterproof nature.

Socks are often an overlooked item by many people. I

usually ware a Keen water shoe if I am going to be in a wet climate, which allows for easy drying of my feet. This principle is difficult if you are in a cold weather climate or prefer to wear boots/sneakers. Having a dry pair of socks to put on, even if your shoes are wet, can save your feet a ton of problems. When I was in the Coast Guard I would often take an extra pair of socks with me on patrols just incase my feet happened to wet. Having your feet wet and inside your shoes can lead to terrible skin deterioration resulting in a condition called "trench foot". This occurs when the feet are wet for an extended period of time and can cause an itchy/burning sensation accompanied by swelling and pain. The blisters that can form by the deterioration of the skin can be quite painful as well. The best way to prevent this is to dry your feet often and at the bare minimum…change your socks every few hours. I suggest having at least 4-6 extra pairs of socks ready to go in your kit.

In addition, it is always good to have emergency cash on hand. During disasters ATM's and banks will likely be closed and your access to money could be limited. Having a reserve of money could be a great asset in the days after a disaster.

Shaun E. Allen

7 THE DISASTER ACTION PLAN

The disaster action plan is where all of the different steps in preparation that we have covered come together and culminate in an easy to follow set of instructions that will give guidance on what to do in the event of a disaster. The plan should be kept as simple as possible and practiced so that it will become second nature. Some people view the plan as a kind of flow chart. For example, if A and B happen then do C. This is a great way to organize a plan and ensures that everyone is on the same page. There are opposing views that argue a flow chart approach is too strict and does not allow for adaptation. This is a warranted concern and I suggest that the flow chart is utilized only as a basic format to make the plan easier to follow but you must also understand that unforeseen things do happen and adaptation to the situation is a must.

By having an easy to follow plan, individuals are more likely to fall back on the plan in times of panic and will have the tendency to make better decisions based on what they have practiced. Practice is the key and as stated before, you cannot expect to perform well during an emergency if the plan is only on paper and has never been practiced.

Get Organized

Organization is very important and can be accomplished by designing a simple information sheet that has locations of safe meeting areas, names, addresses and telephone numbers of family or friends that play a role in the disaster action plan, as well as other important contact information. This paper should be placed near telephones for easy reference. There should also be a copy at your place of work and if you have children, a copy should be included in their school files. Everyone in the household should know who to contact when there is a disaster, especially if family members are separated. The emergency contact person can be utilized as a central hub to help relay important information about the status and location of family members that are caught in a disaster and can't make it to the predetermined meeting location. This person/persons should be outside of your residential area if possible because it is often easier to make calls out of a disaster area than it is to call within a disaster area. Also, make sure that this person is willing to help. They should be aware that they are the contact person for the family in the event that a disaster strikes. This might make them more likely to be near the phone when they are aware of a disaster occurring in your area. There is also a way to let family members know that you are safe by registering your information on a website maintained by the Red Cross. This can be done during or post disaster. It is called *Safe and Well* and is searchable registry that allows family and friends to determine the status of loved ones by entering information into an online database.

The safe meeting location should be decided upon as a family and should include locations for meeting in the house, outside of the house, and a distant location that is away from the house.

The location inside of the house should be an inner room that is well constructed. This could be a basement room, den, or specifically designed safe room. Remember what was covered in the special needs section with regard to mobility and age of family members- the safe location within the home might need to be adjusted as the needs change. This location is utilized for those sudden emergencies such as power outages, severe weather, or any other situation where sheltering inside of the home is advisable. If you do have special needs within the home, this part of the disaster action plan is where you would want to assign another family member to assist this individual if at all possible.

The safe location outside of the house should also be decided upon as a family and should be a location that is a safe distance from the home. This can include locations such as the mailbox, end of driveway, street corner, or geographical location (NW corner of property). This location is important to utilize when the need arises that you must immediately evacuate your home due to an identified danger. This can include fire, smoke, or structural damage to the home. You may be asking *why* have a designated meeting location and not just make it a point to get out the house? Well, imagine that your house is on fire and the smoke detectors have woken you up in the middle of the night. The fire is intense and your immediate instinct is to get out of the house. You run out onto you front lawn and turn around to view the ever increasing inferno. At that moment, you panic; you have family members that are still inside--so you think. Unknown to you, they have escaped out of a rear facing window and are safe in the backyard. You run back inside of the home in an attempt to rescue them but are overcome by the toxic smoke and killed…you died a hero trying to save your family. I agree--a little dramatic, but this scenario does happen and it is both tragic and unfortunate because it could have been prevented. Besides the obvious that you should *NEVER* reenter a burning home once you have made it out, having a predetermined location to meet could have insured that all family members were accounted for. You could replay the same scenario except for this time everyone knows to meet at the end of the driveway. As you realize that there might be family members still inside, you see them emerge from behind the house, heading for the predetermined meeting place. It's a small detail but can make a huge difference.

A location should also be decided that is well away from the home. This could be a family or friends house, community center, fire or police station, designated public shelter or any other place that can be utilized as a meeting area. The idea is if the family is scattered when a disaster occurs and it is impossible to get back to the home due to safety or other reason, this location can serve to reassemble the family. Anytime you are separated from family members and are forced to utilize this option, it should also include attempting to call other members of your family or the emergency contact person to advise them of your status and that you are heading to the safe location, or of your current location and your decision to remain there. Remember, it is important that whatever your action, you want to try to notify your family or the emergency contact if at all possible. It is also important to notify your family or the emergency contact when you change your decided plan of action. The goal is to keep your other family members as informed as possible through direct phone conversations with them or through the emergency contact. Situations when this scenario might play out could be during sudden large disasters like wildfires, severe weather events, or manmade disasters that affect a large geographical area, especially when they occur during working hours when the family is not necessarily together.

Your Children and the Schools

If you do not have children, this section may be of little use to you but STILL read it! The information can be passed on to friends and other family members that do have children to ensure that they are prepared with regard to their children and schools.

It is quite frightening for parents when they have

children in schools and a large disaster occurs. This heartbreaking scenario played out in May of 2013 when a large EF5 tornado (Enhanced Fujita Scale of Tornado Intensity) ripped through Moore Oklahoma killing seven school children at their elementary school. The anxiety of parents not knowing if their child was dead or alive had to be tremendous. The emotions that followed after finding out that their child was among those killed is unknown to most and can never be described in words. When humans are put in the path of one of the strongest events in nature, unfortunately there are fatalities. The school did have a tornado emergency action plan and it was followed, but it did not have above ground tornado safe rooms. The fact that a school full of children was directly hit by an EF5 tornado (winds over 200 mph) and there were *only* seven fatalities is remarkable. *Note: This tornado was 2.6 miles wide and had winds that approached the 300 mph mark.*

There are many other types of disasters that occur all over the country and can involve schools or at least take place during school hours. When this happens, it can be a source of confusion and panic for parents that frantically rush to the schools to get their children. It is important that as a parent you inquire about your child's school and the emergency action plan. Important things to note are whether the children are to remain at the school and shelter in place or if they are to be released to arriving parents. Making sure your child's student file is updated with important contact numbers that reflect the contact numbers in you family's disaster action plan is also important. Talk with your child about the school's policy and reassure them that you understand exactly what will be happening during an emergency and to follow all the instructions of the educational staff. If they understand that you know exactly what they will be doing during an emergency while they are in school, it will help alleviate some of the potential anxiety that could present itself by you not being there when a disaster occurs. Your disaster action plan should account for the actions that your child's school will take during an emergency. It is always a scary situation when there is a disaster and you are separated from your child. Understanding the school's policy will give you some peace of mind.

Sample Emergency Action Plan (information sheet)

EMERGENCY CONTACT

Name:

City of Residence:

Contact Number:

SECONDARY EMERGENCY CONTACT

Name:

City of Residence:

Contact Number:

FAMILY MEMBER CONTACT NUMBERS

Father-   Cell: Work:

Mother-   Cell: Work:

Brother-   Cell: Work:

Sister-   Cell: Work:

…continue with other family members

SAFE MEETING AREAS

Location inside of the home:

Location outside of the home:

Distant location(s) if unsafe to return home:

OTHER IMPORTANT INFORMATION

Veterinarian number:

Closest hospital information:

Fire Department number: (usually 911)

Police Department number: (usually 911)

Local Red Cross number:

Regional FEMA office number:

Insurance Company Information:

Children's school number:

The above information sheet is a basic template guide for the information that you can utilize to help formulate your plan. Again, you should add other pertinent information as you see fit. As you can see, it is a very simple sheet that can be easily referenced when the need for action arises.

This sheet will be referenced when you run through different disaster scenarios as well since it contains all of the contact numbers and locations of the safe meeting areas.

Ready, Set, Action

You can start by running through small-scale disasters that require you to meet in the home or right outside of the home in the designated safe areas. For example, you could plan a scenario that involves a fire in the kitchen or a sudden severe storm. All family members are required to take action and assemble in the proper predetermined safe area. This is a good time to figure out if someone is going to need assistance and to assign responsibilities to another family member to assist this individual in making it to the safe area. You can also practice disasters that you and your family have already identified as being more likely to occur in your location. Once you get the basics down and different family members are comfortable with their responsibilities, you can start incorporating larger disaster scenarios including being separated from the onset. This type of disaster is harder to practice but a good table top discussion of what each would do will get the members of your family thinking. You can give them a disaster scenario where they are at various locations and see how well they can describe their way to the safe meeting area. You can even get your emergency contact involved to field phone calls so they will understand what information they will be receiving. The basic information that should be relayed is your location, status (injured or not) and your planned action (staying put or moving to a meeting area). This may seem pretty silly but if you have children in the home, it will get them comfortable with calling the emergency contact and giving information. (**Note:** family members should understand that it is important to check in with the emergency contact every hour or so if possible to see if there is any updates from other family members).

It is also a good idea that you get a map of the area so that everyone can start getting familiar with the various streets and to gain better directional awareness. After a major disaster, towns and cities can look quite different due to the destruction often found in the aftermath and individuals can easily become disoriented if they rely only on landmarks and buildings to find their way around.

You can make the scenarios interesting especially if

you have taken a first aid course. You can incorporate different injuries to assess how well you and your family members are able to manage these injuries in a disaster situation.

When you are practicing these scenarios…HAVE FUN! Learning is always better when it is interesting and enjoyable. Nobody wants to feel like they are being forced to participate. Hopefully your family members will understand and appreciate the importance of being prepared for disasters.

….a final note

There is always the chance that you during or post disaster that you will be alone and will not be able to make contact with any of the emergency contacts or other family members. You will need to remain calm and take care of yourself. Try to get to the designated safe meeting area if possible and trust that your family members are doing the same. Don't panic and make bad decisions that could cause you to become part of the problem. It can be a scary situation not knowing the location and status of your family members and that is why trying to stay in contact with them directly or via the emergency contact is so important. If you cannot get in contact with anyone, slow down, think, and make good decisions in order to stay safe until you can make contact.

AUTHOR'S NOTES

I feel that the easiest way to define it is: any event, natural or manmade, that causes damage and suffering, and requires some sort of outside assistance. This definition does have certain limitations as well. Countries and regions can have different triggers for assistance and sometimes it can even be a political decision-
http://www.pitt.edu/~epi2170/lecture15/sld007.htm

Natural disasters can include weather events; such as hurricanes and floods, and geological events; such as earthquakes and volcanoes. Manmade disasters can include industrial, environmental, and transportation incidents, as well as terrorism- Principle Causes of Disasters
http://webworld.unesco.org/safeguarding/en/txt_sini.ht m

It is an ever present reality that disasters, both natural and manmade, are on the rise globally- NASA Earth Observatory
http://earthobservatory.nasa.gov/Features/RisingCost/ris

ing_cost5.php
The Research Institute of Economic, Trade and Industry
http://www.rieti.go.jp/jp/publications/dp/11e023.pdf

Flooding is the most prominent disaster in the United States- Federal Emergency Management Agency/ National Flood Insurance Program
http://www.floodsmart.gov/floodsmart/pages/media_res ources/stats.jsp

The United States is also unique with regard to tornados in that approximately 70% of tornados that occur on entire earth rip right through the center of the country- National Oceanic and Atmospheric Administration National Climate Data Center
http://www.ncdc.noaa.gov/oa/climate/severeweather/tor nadoes.html

A year later when "Superstorm Sandy" approached the same area, many did not evacuate because they expected the same result- USA Today *Officials fear that many won't evacuate for hurricane sandy*
http://www.usatoday.com/story/news/nation/2012/10/ 28/hurricane-sandy-wont-evacuate/1662755/

Some say it is the "crying wolf" syndrome where many false alarms can result in disregarding such warnings- The New York Times The Opinion Pages (Randolph, B.)
http://www.nytimes.com/roomfordebate/2011/08/29/

There was a series of storms that caused evacuation of the city multiple times and yet the number of people that evacuated remained almost the same each time- *Hurricane Evacuation Behavior* (Baker, E.), Department of Geology Florida State University
http://www.bama.ua.edu/~jcsenkbeil/gy4570/Baker%20

91%20evacuation.pdf
Lower Southeast Florida Hurricane Evacuation Study
University of South Florida Department of Psychology
http://www.csc.noaa.gov/hes/docs/hes/LOWER_SEFL
ORIDA_HES.pdf

The elderly, people living in poverty, and many pet owners were not considered in the coordination of the mass evacuations taking place all through New Orleans and surrounding areas and consequently were left behind- *National Study on Carless and Special Needs Evacuation Planning : A Literature Review,* University of New Orleans Transportation Center
http://www.uno.edu/cola/departments/plus/docs/Carles
sEvacuationPlanning.pdf
Back Ground On Hurricane Katrina
http://www.dosomething.org/tipsandtools/background-
katrina#

The stress of the disaster is often amplified in this population and their coping mechanisms may not handle the effects of disasters as well as middle-aged individuals- Agency for toxic Substance and Disease Registry, *Relocation: Relocation Stress*
http://www.doh.state.fl.us/family/mch/disasterpreparedn
ess/RelocationStress.pdf

If the water entered through a damaged portion of the roof, you would be covered, but since it hit the ground it is now considered surface water and may not be covered, especially if you do not have flood protection in your policy- Charlie Long, Nationwide Insurance Adjuster involving large claims, specifically fire related incidents.

FEMA suggest that you have at least 1 gallon of water per person per day in order to sustain them for three

days- Federal Emergency Management Agency
http://www.ready.gov/water

Primitive camping techniques requires you to dig a hole (catholes) at least 6-8 inches deep in the ground so that you can completely cover the human waste with dirt when you are done- *Principle 3: Dispose of Waste Properly,* Leave No Trace
http://lnt.org/learn/principle-3

This occurs when the feet are wet for an extended period of time and can cause an itchy/burning sensation accompanied by swelling and pain- *What is Trench Foot,* wiseGEEK
http://www.wisegeek.org/what-is-trench-foot.htm

This heartbreaking scenario played out in May of 2013 when a large EF5 (Enhanced Fujita Scale of Tornado Intensity) tornado ripped through Moore Oklahoma killing seven school children at their elementary school- AP The Big Story
http://bigstory.ap.org/article/oklahoma-schools-hit-tornado-had-no-safe-rooms

USEFUL WEBSITES

http://www.fema.gov/ -everything you wanted to know about the Federal Emergency Management Agency. The site has a lot of good information about disaster preparedness. You can also find information about your regional FEMA office.

http://environment.nationalgeographic.com/environment/natural-disasters/ -this is a great educational site that is very interactive. It teaches about specific disasters and what you should do to survive them. The information found on this site can be incorporated in your scenarios to make them disaster specific.

http://www.nasponline.org/resources/crisis_safety/naturaldisaster_ho.aspx -if you have children in you home, this site is a must visit. This is a huge resource for learning how to help children cope with disasters. It gives ideas of things you can do for specific disasters to help ease their fears and anxiety.

http://www.kelty.com -this is the site where you can find my favorite backpack. They also have quite a bit of other camping and hiking gear.

http://www.noaa.gov/   -good site to learn about severe weather systems, specifically hurricanes. It also has information on global climate change and ocean water temperature changes.

http://www.firesafetytips.com/ -information on fire safety. The site gives basic training on fire situations that you can use in your scenarios. It also has information on different escape systems that can be installed on the second floors of residential homes. WARNING- there is an annoying siren sound when you navigate from page to page…you might want to turn the volume down on your computer.

http://www.keenfootwear.com/us/en/   -by far the best shoes on earth for water and hiking!

http://www.redcross.org/ -great site for disaster preparedness. This site can give you information on how you can help by giving donations or volunteering your time. During disasters, specific information on shelters and other useful information can be found here.

SUGGESTED ACTIVITIES FOR THE FAMILY

There are many activities that you and your family can participate in that can help give you certain skills and mindsets to better handle disaster situations. We have already covered some of these, such as taking **first aid**, **CPR**, and **fire safety** classes. The following are a few others that can help develop skills that can aid in becoming better prepared for disasters.

Boy Scouts and Girl Scouts- These organizations are great to get children of the family involved in. They can teach valuable lessons about safety, teamwork, and problem solving. Many of the skills learned can directly be applied to disaster situations. (Parents should consider becoming involved as a scout leader...you may learn something)

Camping- "Roughing" it as a family can teach valuable lessons as well. Choosing to be slightly inconvenienced by not having the creature comforts of electricity and heating/air conditioning can make the sudden shock of not having these things during and after a disaster a little more bearable. You can also practice your gourmet cooking skills over an open fire or on you small camping stove.

Go Hiking- Get out and explore nature! Besides helping you get some much needed fresh air, it plays a more important role in that it is great exercise and gets you used to putting some miles on your feet. You never know when a disaster may require you to log several miles on foot.

Take Swim Classes- This is very important for those in your family that have a fear of water or cannot swim. There may be a situation in a disaster where being able to swim can be the difference between life and death. Remember, flooding is the most prominent natural disaster in the United Stated, so it would make sense to learn how to swim.

Learn a Skill Specific for Disaster Situations- There are a number of skills that can be applied in a disaster situation but require a little effort.

Amateur Radio (also known as HAM radio) can be a

hobby that plays an important function with regard to communications during a disaster. This requires you to become licensed by the Federal Communications Commission (FCC) but can be quite useful in staying connected to other licensed family members via these radios since they utilize UF, VHF, and UHF radio waves and do not rely on telephone lines/cell towers, which are often rendered useless post disasters.

Survival Classes- Survival classes are offered in many regions of the country that teach participants to rely on very little in order to survive. This can teach individuals what natural foods are safe to eat, how to build shelters, primitive hunting skills, and how to start a fire with nothing more than sticks. This may be a little more extreme than some of the other activities, but if you can learn to survive with nothing, just think what you can do with you disaster supplies at the ready.

ABOUT THE AUTHOR

Shaun Allen grew up as a child having "Wild, Wonderful, West Virginia" as his playground. He is an avid outdoorsman and sports enthusiast.

At age 19 he enlisted in the United States Coast Guard and was stationed on South Padre Island Texas where he was engaged in counter narcotic, counter migrant, and search and rescue operations.

After leaving the Coast Guard he achieved certifications as both a Florida State Fire Fighter and Florida State Emergency Medical Technician-Paramedic. He has worked over a decade in the Emergency Medical Services field, 6 years of which was as a firefighter/paramedic for Pasco County Fire Rescue.

His education includes an Associates of Applied Science in Emergency Medical Services, a Bachelor of Science in Fire Science, and a Master of Science in Emergency Services Management.

Notes

Notes

Notes

www.ingramcontent.com/pod-product-compliance
Lightning Source LLC
Chambersburg PA
CBHW070556290526
45790CB00002B/718